THE NATURE KIDS GUIDE TO AXOLOTLS

DAVID ANDERSON

LP Media Inc. Publishing
Text copyright © 2026 by LP Media Inc.
All rights reserved.

For information address LP Media Inc. Publishing,
30012 Variolite St NW, Princeton MN 55371
www.lpmedia.org

Publication Data

Axolotls
The Nature Kid's Guide to Axolotls — First edition.

Summary: "Learn all about Axolotls, the Nature Kid Way"
— Provided by publisher.

ISBN: 979-8-89818-109-3

[1. Axolotls - Non-Fiction] I. Title.

Title: The Nature Kid's Guide to Axolotls

CONTENTS

LAKE LIFE

Axolotls once lived in two lakes called Xochimilco and Chalco. Lake Chalco was drained long ago. Now wild axolotls only live in Lake Xochimilco.

Splash! A pink Axolotl floats in dark water. Its feathery gills wave.

Axolotls are **amphibians**. They live their whole lives in water. Most amphibians grow up and move to land. But axolotls stay in the water forever.

Wild Axolotls need cool, calm lakes. The water must be fresh, not salty. Plants grow thick on the bottom. The lakes feel quiet and still.

Axolotls like shallow water. They rest on muddy lake floors. Rocks and plants give them places to hide. The cool water keeps them healthy and happy.

MEXICAN
MAGIC

Swoosh! An axolotl glides past tall plants. It's a pet Axolotl that lives in an aquarium.

Axolotls live naturally in only one place on Earth. They are found in Mexico.

Wild axolotls live in Lake Xochimilco. This lake is near Mexico City. It is the only home for wild axolotls.

No other country has wild axolotls. They do not live in any other lake. Mexico is their only true home.

Lake Xochimilco sits about 7,000 feet above sea level in a mountain valley.

SMALL SWIMMERS

Snap! A small axolotl rests on a rock. It fits in your hand.

Axolotls are not very big. Most adults grow to only about nine inches long. That is about as long as a banana.

They also weigh very little. A full-grown axolotl weighs around eight ounces. That is lighter than a can of soup.

Young axolotls are even tinier. Baby axolotls are about half an inch long when they hatch. They grow slowly over many months.

An axolotl's body is usually as wide as its head. This helps them gulp food fast.

FUNKY FRILLS
DID YOU KNOW?
Axolotls can regrow damaged gills. New ones grow back in just a few weeks.

Whoosh! An axolotl swims by with fluffy stalks framing its face.

Axolotls have six feathery stalks on their heads. These are called **gills**. The gills stick out like tiny trees. They help axolotls breathe underwater.

Blood flows through these gills. This is what makes them look pink or red. The gills take **oxygen** from the water. Then the oxygen goes into the blood.

Axolotls wave their gills back and forth. This brings fresh water to them and gives them more oxygen. Healthy gills are fluffy and full.

SUPER SENSORS

Click! An axolotl turns its head. It senses something nearby.

Axolotls have small eyes. They do not have eyelids. They cannot see very well.

They use other senses. Axolotls feel the water move. This helps them find food. It helps them stay safe too.

Axolotls can smell well. They smell the water. This helps them find worms to eat.

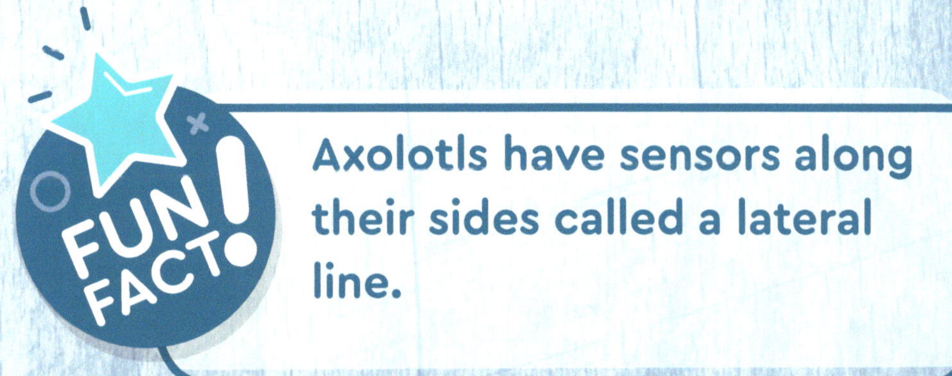

SLIMY SKIN
14

Squeak! The axolotl floats gently, its wet skin glistening softly.

Axolotls have slimy skin. A special coating covers their body. This slime is called **mucus**.

The mucus helps keep them safe. It makes axolotls slippery. This makes it hard for predators to grab them.

The slime also keeps germs away. It works like a shield. Axolotls make fresh mucus all the time.

Axolotl skin is so thin you can see their blood vessels through it in places.

WORM LOVERS

Chomp! An axolotl snaps at a wiggly worm below. Dinner is served!

Axolotls eat worms, insects, and small fish. They also eat snails and tiny shrimp. These foods give them energy to grow.

Worms are a favorite food. Axolotls find them by smell and suck them into their mouths quickly.

Axolotls eat at night. They search the lake bottom for food and swallow their meals whole without chewing.

Axolotls sometimes eat tadpoles and even will eat smaller axolotls!

GULP IT

Axolotls must be within one inch of prey for their suction feeding to work.

Slurp! An axolotl opens its mouth wide underwater.

Axolotls have tiny teeth that are used for gripping, not chewing. These small bumps cannot break down food.

Axolotls use suction to eat. They open their mouths very fast. This creates a vacuum that pulls food inside. Water and prey rush in together.

This happens in a split second. The axolotl snaps its jaws shut. Then it swallows the food whole. Small fish, tadpoles, and bugs all go down the same way.

To catch prey, axolotls wait very still. Then they lunge forward with their mouths open wide.

WATCH OUT

A large fish swims close. The axolotl stays very still.

Axolotls have **predators** in their lake home. Large fish like tilapia and carp eat them. Birds also hunt axolotls from above.

Herons wade in shallow water. They use sharp beaks to catch axolotls. Egrets use this same trick to hunt them too.

Long ago, people brought new fish to the lake. These fish eat axolotl eggs and babies. This makes life much harder for wild axolotls.

Carp were brought to Mexico from Asia over one hundred years ago.

HIDE AWAY

Swoosh! An axolotl darts behind a rock and hides in the shadows.

Axolotls hide to stay safe. They squeeze under rocks and logs. These dark spaces keep them out of sight.

Plants help axolotls hide too. Thick weeds make good cover. Axolotls also blend in with muddy lake bottoms.

When scared, axolotls stay very still. They do not move until danger passes. Hiding and camouflage help axolotls stay safe.

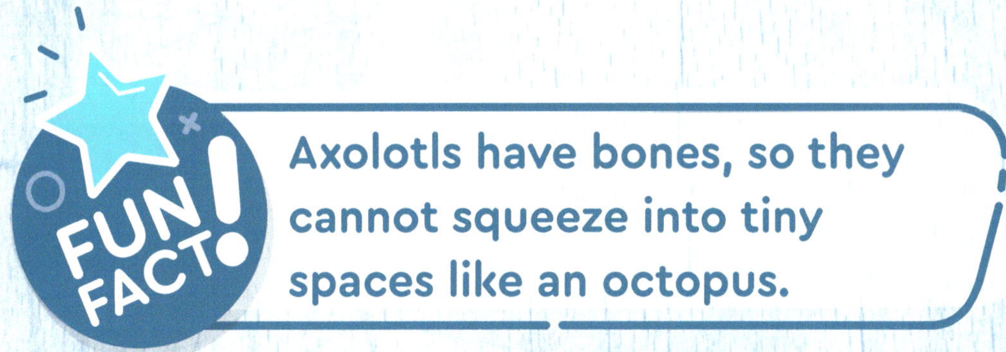

WIGGLY WALKERS

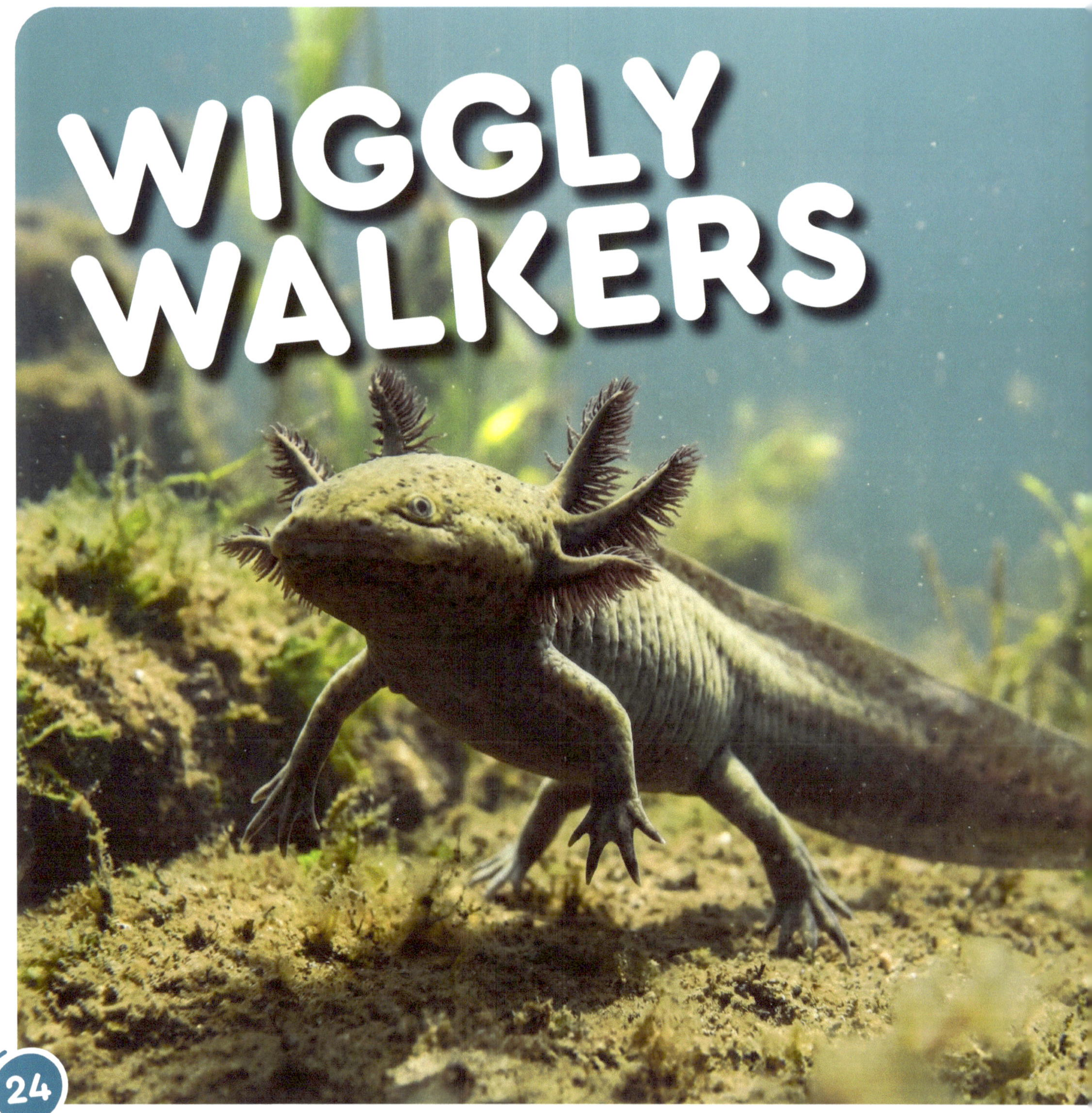

Thump! An axolotl pushes off the lake bottom with its legs.

Axolotls have four short legs. Each leg has tiny toes. They use these legs to walk along the lake floor.

Axolotls are not fast walkers. They take slow, careful steps. Their legs push through mud and sand.

Axolotls can also swim. They wiggle their long tails from side to side and glide throught the water.

Axolotls have four toes on their front legs and five toes on their back legs. That is 18 toes in all!

NIGHT SHIFT

Crunch! A young axolotl crawls over gravel at night, ready to explore.

Axolotls are most active at night. They move around when the lake is dark. Daytime is for resting in hidden spots.

At night, axolotls search for food. They walk slowly along the lake bottom, gills waving as they explore.

Darkness helps axolotls stay safer. Predators have a harder time seeing them, so night is the best time for axolotls to be out.

Axolotls have no eyelids, so they rely on darkness to rest their eyes. Bright light can stress them out.

ALONE TIME

Shhh! A quiet axolotl floats by itself. This creature likes being alone.

Axolotls live alone. They do not form groups or families. Each axolotl stays by itself in the lake.

Axolotls do not play together or groom each other. Being alone is normal for them.

Sometimes axolotls meet. They may bump into each other while looking for food. But they do not stay together long.

Axolotls may bite other axolotls if they get too close. This is why they like space.

DANCE TIME

Swirl! Two axolotls circle each other in the dark water.

Axolotls mate in water. A male bumps a female with his nose. He swims in circles around her.

The male drops tiny packets on the lake floor. These packets hold special cells. The female picks them up.

Axolotls can mate at one to two years old. They often mate in cool water. This happens in winter or spring.

A female axolotl can lay between 100 and 1,000 eggs after mating. She then attaches them to plants.

TINY LARVAE

Axolotl larvae have tiny stick-like parts near their heads that help them balance until their legs grow.

Cute! Tiny eggs sit on lake plants. Baby axolotls grow inside.

Axolotl eggs are small and round. Each egg is clear like jelly. You can see the baby growing inside.

A female can lay hundreds of eggs at once. She attaches them to plants or rocks. The eggs stick there safely.

Baby axolotls hatch after about two weeks. These tiny babies are called larvae. Each larva is smaller than a grain of rice.

Larvae have no legs at first. They grow front legs, then back legs.

SOLO START

Bye! A mother axolotl swims away from her eggs. She will not return.

Axolotl parents do not care for their young. The mother lays her eggs. Then she leaves. She does not guard them. She does not feed them.

The father swims away too. He does not help at all. Baby axolotls must live on their own.

New babies find their own food. They eat tiny animals in the water. No adult shows them how to hunt. They learn by themselves.

This solo start is normal for axolotls. Many water animals raise babies this way.

REGENERATION SUPERSTARS
36

Snap! An axolotl loses a leg. It will grow back!

Axolotls can regrow body parts. They grow new legs. They grow new tails. They grow new gills. They can even regrow parts of their heart and brain!

This skill is called regeneration. The new parts work just like the old ones.

Scientists study axolotls. They want to learn how they do this. No other animal can regrow so many parts.

An axolotl can regrow the same limb over one hundred times during its life. Each new limb works perfectly.

AXOLOTL CARE CREW

Pet Axolotls can live 10 to 15 years with proper care. They need tanks with gentle water flow.

Swoosh! An axolotl glides through clean water.

Lake Xochimilco has become dirty and small. People are working hard to save it.

Scientists and local farmers are cleaning the water. They are removing pollution and trash. They are also getting rid of fish that eat axolotls. These fish do not belong in the lake.

People are building safe spaces in the water. They add plants that axolotls like. They create places for them to hide and lay eggs. Some groups are raising baby axolotls. Then they release them into the clean parts of the lake.

They want Axolotls to survive in the wild for a long time.

GLOSSARY

amphibians
Animals that can live both in water and on land.

gills
Feathery body parts that help animals breathe underwater.

oxygen
A gas in air and water that animals need to breathe and stay alive.

mucus
A slimy coating that covers and protects an animal's body.

predators
Animals that hunt and eat other animals.